Skunks!

by David T. Greenberg

Illustrated by
Lynn Munsinger

Megan Tingley Books

L|B Little, Brown and Company
Boston New York London

Of all the world's uncs
I've got the two sweetest skunks
I won't fool ya
They're Jessica and Julia

Love, Duvy

For Kendall Anne and her big sister, Alex

L. M.

Text copyright © 2001 by David T. Greenberg
Illustrations copyright © 2001 by Lynn Munsinger

First Edition
Library of Congress Cataloging-in-Publication Data

Greenberg, David (David T.).
    Skunks! / by David T. Greenberg ; illustrated by Lynn Munsinger.
    — 1st ed.
      p. cm.
    "Megan Tingley Books."
    Summary: Suggests all kinds of silly, smelly things that one could do
with skunks.
    ISBN 0-316-32606-2
    [1. Skunks — Fiction. 2. Stories in rhyme.] I. Munsinger, Lynn, ill.
II. Title.
PZ8.3.G755 Sk 2001
[E] — dc21   00-026883

E
Gree

10 9 8 7 6 5 4 3 2

TWP

Printed in Singapore

The illustrations for this book were done in watercolor.
The text was set in BeLucian Book.

The stunkiest stank ever to stink
The stankiest stink to stunk
Far worse than a moldy garbage can
When you reach down and scoop out the gunk

A million times worse than
octopus armpits
Or sniffing an elephant trunk

Is the galling, appalling,
truly enthralling
Glorious stink of a skunk!

Sing songs to the stink of a skunk
Ring gongs to the stink of a skunk
Ding dongs to the stink of a skunk
The glorious stink of a skunk

But the stink of a skunk
I always have thunk
Is more than a sweet bouquet
There are numerous other things (that a punk)
Can do with the heavenly spray

A spray that can stun even squirrels
Almost radioactive
Which for normal boys 'n' girls
Makes it quite attractive

First of all, it's valid
To keep a skunk as a pet
And spray your family's salad
In place of a vinaigrette

It's okay to spray on the toothbrushes
Of everyone in your family
It's okay to spray in the dresser drawer
Where your sister keeps her pajamily

Skunks make excellent hats
Really cozy undies
Whip their spray like Cool Whip
And slather ice cream sundies

A giant mound of skunks
Makes an incredibly comfortable bed
In place of fluffy slippers
A pair of skunks instead

Skunks make superior sprinklers
For watering your grass
Pump their tails several times
Spray insects with their gas

Skunks for Super Soakers
(It's okay to play inside)
A hovercraft of squirting skunks
Take it for a ride

Get married to a skunk
And save a thousand bucks
He can carbonate all of the wedding drinks
And won't require a tux

Punk rocker skunks, bizarrely tattooed
Ninja skunks with attitude
Sumo skunks scarfing food
Skunks with purple Mohawks, dude

They're perfect for powdering noses
With their very own built-in hair
They're perfect for washing windows
With their very own built-in sprayer

Why can't Santa's sled
Be pulled by skunks instead?
Reindeer are lovable fellas
But skunks have jet propellas

Choose skunk gas at the gas station
To fill your limousine
It's high-octane and unleaded
And will make your car run clean

Place a skunk
In Brother's bunk
Drop one in his bath
Kerplunk

Climb into your skunkmobile
Snap a skunk salute
Then rocket out of the skunk cave
In your super skunker suit

Hyper windshield-wiper skunks
Little baby diaper skunks
(Not only are they likable
They're naturally recyclable)

Skunk-cabbage casserole
Spicy skunk salami

Skunk tornadoes, skunk volcanoes
A giant skunk tsunami

Your neighbors will soon catch wind of the fact
There are skunks in your apartment
And frantically will contact
The Stink Control Department

Antiskunk commandos
Will parachute from jets
With tranquilizer weapons
To neutralize your pets

Ninja skunks will counterattack
Sumo skunks will charge
Blimp skunks overhead
Will drop their skunk discharge

Skunkzilla and Skunk Kong
Will lift their monstrous tails
Aim at the attackers
And spray like spouts of whales

The attackers have been skunked!
And you may rest content
With your loving skunk companions
Who are truly heaven-scent